Sinzibuckwud!

the poet's experiences in, and on the way
to and from, Montreal, Québec, Canada

Rick Lupert

Sinzibuckwud!

Ain't Got No Press

Design, and Layout ~ Rick Lupert
Author and Cover Photos ~ Addie Lupert

Thank you Addie, Brendan, Stephan, The people who thought it would be a good idea to put cheese curds and gravy on top of french fries, The people of New Jersey, Montréal Complètement Cirque, The bunny, and Bernie and Sara Schonbach who enjoyed a week in Allentown with Jude so we could enjoy a week in Montreal with each other.

(818) 904-1021

or

15522 Stagg Street
Van Nuys, CA 91406

or

Rick@PoetrySuperHighway.com

or

PoetrySuperHighway.com

First Edition ~ December, 2010

ISBN: 978-0-9820584-2-8 $12.00

Sin-zi-buck-wud

From the Algonquin: Drawn from wood, as in there is maple sap in the wood and we will draw it out to sweeten the things that go in our mouths.

Not to be confused with sinzibukwouldn't.

To Addie, I mean seriously...

l'Amérique

Foundation

The couples in the airport
who wear matching shirts

so they will be able to find
each other.

Addie and I rely on knowing
what the other looks like.

Are We There Yet?

We are on a plane in Chicago with no pilot.
Do not worry; it is still on the ground.
Earlier, the airport coffee shops were out of ice.
So we are without cold drinks and going nowhere.
Our son screams at his absent bear.

A Cross-Species Relationship is Not Forged

The bunny on the Allentown lawn
is right not to trust me

I would just talk to him about
unpopular wars

and the rising cost
of carrots

Robbers have made away with the grill

I

And so this independence day meal consists
of couscous and mini-quiches.

Thieves have taken our Americana.
The last time I used the word Americana

Was in a poem about Mister T.

II

A truck stops for two minutes
on Springhouse Road.

After a commotion, a sofa
is tossed into the backyard.

Somewhere else in Allentown
criminals are eating barbecue

and not sitting comfortably.

And Now You Know Too Much

It is the fourth of July
and I am wearing American flag
red, white and blue underwear.

Oh no, I wrote this same exact poem
four years ago in Boston.
I need new underwear.

Open

Our son goes up to
a stranger at the fireworks
and says *up*,
meaning pick me up.

We haven't taught him
to be cautious of strangers.
We may never.

Haiku

A bronze breasted bird
on an evergreen tree branch
King of Springhouse Road

Bluetensils

One night
spooning in bed
Addie asks if
there's such a thing
as forking.

Soon every imaginable
utensil is being listed.

When we get to spatula
we pretend to go to sleep.

Whisk.

On The Road Again

The first sign we see on the way to Canada says
"Welcome to New Jersey".
I'll let you draw your own conclusions.

Brunch Trumps Patriotism

All the parking spaces
in Ridgewood, New Jersey

are taken by people come to see
the Fifth of July Parade

Sorry Ridgewood, and America.
We are only here for the giant pancakes

A Poem by Our Empty Stomachs

Addie reads a sign in the parade as
"Junior Band and Bagel corps"
which actually says
"Junior Band and Bugle Corps"
It is clear we have not had breakfast yet

Modern Art

This is the first time I'm writing my poetry
by typing it into the phone while on the go
as opposed to writing it in a journal.

Can you tell? Is my typewriting legible?
Is the automatic spell check making sure
all the words are corrupt?

There are 87 eggs in my flowboob.

There is a town in New York called Coxsackie

There is nothing I could say to
enhance that statement further.

Criminal

Not even my incredible wit and
promises of a small press publishing deal

could talk the New York State Trooper
out of the traffic citation.

Apparently 84 in a 65
is beyond his tolerance.

He says if I pay the fine he'd consider
sending me a few poems

and we leave it at that.

Montreal
un

Upon Seeing George Clinton in Montreal

Last night I exposed Addie to the funk.
When it was all done I said to her

That, my friend, is the funk.

This is what was said to me when
I was first exposed to the funk.

It is a strange thing to refer to your wife as simply
"my friend" when that doesn't quite cover it.

She is like the uber-super friend with
benefits that would be inappropriate to describe
at this time.

Hot, Wet, Hair

Thanks to the humidity and the wind
I now have an up-do.

I discover this in Notre Dame.
Not the one in Paris.

But the one here in Montreal.
It's where I am.

Sinzibuckwud

That's what the Native North Americans
called Maple Syrup.

sinzibuckwud

Literally, drawn from wood.
In any language, the marketing

left something to be desired.

Remembering Boats-Gone-By
For No Reason

Being on a boat tour of the St. Lawrence River
reminds Addie of another boat we toured and

she asks me to help remember where that boat was.
I start to list all the boats we've toured.

There was the Cutty Sark in Greenwich outside London,
dry docked with a museum of mastheads in the hold.

The Queen Mary in Long Beach and it's ghost tour,
complete with sound effects on the lower level.

The decommissioned Russian submarine next to that,
with tiny sleeping quarters for all sized red soldiers.

The Erie Canal Museum built on the boulevard that
used to be the actual canal.

The Revolutionary War-era ship in Boston that sails
once a year on the fourth of July, one of the last

living relics of the revolutionary war.
No wait. Addie stops me. *I think it was a train.*

Addie's Advice on Picking up Grapes with Fondue Forks

You have to go slow and steady
and when it's in the cheese, it's hard to find.

Now go forth and do it.

Still Trying

It is easy to not speak French in Montreal.
The locals switch between it and English

as quickly as breathing.
It is easy to give up quickly when

the woman in the coffee shop responds
to the question *Parlez-vous Anglais?*

with a comforting
Sure do.

La Banquise

We settle down for our first poutine in Montreal
after a day of broken shoes and sweat.

We saw our first parade here today where
an English speaking nine year old stepped on my foot.

I learned for the first time they don't have apologies
in her homeland.

We went on our first boat tour on the St. Lawrence river today.
I knew the name from elementary school geography

but here we were on it learning the difference between
the slow waters of the Old Port and the rough current of

the river that the natives weren't strong enough to navigate.
Tonight as the first poutine arrived the waiter told us

we had to pay first.
We paid first.

The gravy on top of the cheese curds
on top of the French fries.

A Canadian beer chased it down
The kitchen never closes.

Haiku

A broken shoe is
fixed with a stapler and three
pieces of scotch tape

The Right Decision Has Been Made

Addie points out
the Beaver Club
in the guidebook.
I'm so glad I got
into this marriage.

Musée des
Beaux-Arts
de Montreal

We Approach The Museum

A friendly woman guides us from the Metro
to the museum of fine arts. It is a block from
where she works in one of the largest insurance
firms in Montreal. She tells us this is the only place
in the world you can walk the streets at three a.m.
and feel safe. We tell her we will make a point
of waking up then to experience that. Addie is
happy to meet what she calls *a true local*.

There is an underground tunnel connecting the
two buildings of this museum. We look forward
to who we might meet there.

Because We Arrived When it Opened

I am the first one to use the bathroom in the museum.
I know what you're thinking

Oh no...not another poem about
a bathroom in a foreign country.

I really just wanted to comment on how clean it was
but if it will make you feel better, I'll just stop here.

The Artistry of Music Wins Out
Over the Science

Miles Davis recorded the soundtrack to the film
Ascenseur Pour L'Echafaud in one take, live,
while watching the film.

Nothing pre-composed. The music would have
been different if he had come the next day,
and different if he had come the day after that.

On My Second Trip to the Bathroom in the Museum

Ha ha ha just kidding.

Miles Davis, Dead or Alive

The Jazz Festival is extended an extra day for us
with the Miles Davis exhibit. It ends at 1990.

We wonder what happened after that.
It is possible he died, though they don't mention it.

Perhaps, the exhibitors miscalculated the space needed
for the planned exhibit and ran out of room for

the materials depicting his life and/or death after 1990.
There may be a box in the back with a sign in it

that says "Miles Davis is alive and well and living
in Cincinnati, Ohio." Or a different sign that says

"Miles Davis is dead, we're so sorry to have to tell you,
but it is true. We checked and he's definitely not alive."

I find out later he died in 1991.
Much later.

Apologies If This One Isn't For You

We walk up the oddly shaped stairs like John Cleese
in the Ministry of Silly Walks. You either know what
I'm talking about here or you don't.

Saint Cecilia,
John William Waterhouse,
1895

Sleeping in a plush garden chair
      overlooking the sea

while two young maidens
      probably virgins,

play soothing violin serenades
      on their knees.

Man,
      I wish I could afford that.

Forever!! Never!!, Pierre-Eugène-Émile Hébert, 1860

Skeletal Death carries along an attractive young woman, presumably dead. Only in this case Death has a moustache.

It must have been the seventies.

Old Furniture

An ornately decorated
chest of drawers from 1760

with a complex marble top
and wooden drawers,

no straight lines,
gold inlay fixtures, handles,

keyholes and
paintings of flowers.

I'll get you one of these if you want, I tell Addie,
you can put your crap in it.

What crap
she answers.

Domestic Dispute

The painting with the fat baby
prompts the argument about
whether our son's belly is
fat or just big.

Addie says it's just big.

Torso of a Young Woman, Aristide Maillot, 1935

Addie declares one sculpture's title as
Headless Naked Chick despite it's actual title
Torso of a Young Woman.
Who's writing this book anyway?

Upon Seeing Pablo Picasso's Painting *The Head of a Musketeer*, 1969

And the ass of a Shriner
I always say.

Portrait of Maria Carbonate, Salvador Dali, 1925

We see a Salvador Dali
which is not at all surreal.
Which is kind of surreal.

Montreal
deux

In reference to an earlier undocumented conversation in which we assumed the word *incendiary* on the fire stations had something to do with fire

In the chocolate shop on Rue St. Denis
I ask the waiter if he would set my dessert on fire

since I had just seen him serve another crepe
in that manner.

It is too late he says.
It is too bad I say, *everything is better flambé.*

Does that mean fire, Addie asks,
because I don't see flambé stations anywhere.

A Day of Excess

The pictures on the website do not do justice to
the meals Stephan prepares at our bed and breakfast.
French toast and fresh fruit drizzled in something
golden and sweet.

We spend the day in museums looking at art
from all time periods. A trip to the Atwater Market
entrusts a boy at the cheese shop to prepare us
a plate of his favorites.

A fresh baguette and an iced tea later and
we are in business. We could eat cheese in prison
and it would be like a vacation.

More art and then an hour of wondering what to do
which was really an excuse to do nothing.
A walk up a street, closed off, perhaps permanently
for whatever needs the word *festival* after it that week.

There are men holding hands in the street. There are women
walking arm in arm. This is the Latin Quarter and the artists
are unappreciated in their tents...some of them anyway.
Did I mention we gave five dollars American to the

woman with the clip board who asked us if we
had heard of *the missing children?* It is true.
We Metro it back to one place and walk up Rue St. Denis.
This is the street of our content. This is where the excess happens.

In no need of dinner we have tapas.
Things are done with potatoes and asparagus.
One of us is seated on a swing.

We walk to the cinema to determine if the films are dubbed or
subtitled. Nothing tells us anything. So it's back to the street and
Juliette Et Chocolat where caramel crepe, peanut butter brownie,
and chocolate mojito are brought to our table.

Much of this goes into our mouths. Wisely, not all of it.
We forgo a beer stop as our stomachs are threatening
to buy one-way tickets without us.
Two important things are said on the way back.

One, after a glance into a crowded bar, blues musician on stage,
is *if only we were night people.* The second, after a week of
dealing with exploded pen residue in the backpack, is
Yes, the keys are in the pocket that turns me blue.

We return to our room,
white as the day we were born,
no idea what we'll do tomorrow.

With Apologies to Gershwin

Summertime and it is okay to be alive.
A fish jumped out of the St. Lawrence River.
Gravity and a fish eating crane sent it back under.
As for cotton, I am wearing some and I am not tall.

My father is doing well for himself and my mother,
her eyes serve her well. So be quiet children,
The film is about to commence and do not let the noir
images sadden you.

At a certain point later on, before twelve o'clock noon,
I will get up out of this seat with a song slipping from my mouth.
I will wear an outfit composed of feathers.
I will take to the sky.

Until such time, I am invincible!
Father and mother are willing
to do whatever it takes.

As I mentioned,
he can afford to send me plane tickets.
and she, at least her old pictures,
are pleasing on the wall.

I will not ask you to be quiet again.
You still have that new person smell.
Do not let the water
fall from your eyes.

In the Montreal History and Archaeology Museum

Addie is too tired to read all the explanations,
so I point to a broken plate and say that it is
a broken plate.

And I point to dirt in the same showcase
from the original soil of this place and I say
that it is dirt.

She says that she didn't say she couldn't
see objects. She is just too tired to read.
I say *Yes, but that dirt is in French.*

With the Chinese

We stop for tea in Old Port.
It is not as wet in the air outside
and it is hard to resist a tea in any country.

A room full of tea pots, Asian music and
air conditioning. They are out of the vegetarian
buns but that is okay. A tofu roll is on the way.

They do not usually bring honey with the tea
but they will inquire and with a quick question,
a nod and, yes, the Darjeeling will be sweetened.

A tea comes, two pots and a cup.
Hot water is poured into one pot
and from that pot into another

and then into the cup.
The cup is emptied onto the first pot.
The tea flows down the edges of the pot

into the wooden plate.
It is done again, except this time
the tea stays in the cup

and is then lifted to the mouth
where it is poured in and becomes
part of the digestive system.

A conversation occurs
about the strength of the
impending Darjeeling.

The woman has lived longer than me
and knows what is right for tea.
But I know what I like.

Eventually an infuser is brought to me.
I steep at my discretion
between chicken that is not chicken

and unidentifiable greens.
A thousand wooden Buddhas
survey the experience.

History of Everywhere

In Old Town everything is new
or a reminder of the old.

A 1905 building houses
a McDonald's.

Ruins are
a museum.

At certain places they want to turn my money
into other money.

North of the St Lawrence a boy convinces a girl
to speak with a southern accent.

A woman I know sleeps in
a brown chair.

Ice melts in a cup
nearby.

Some are wearing shoes.
Some wish they weren't.

A display of lights and manmade pasta
is in the future.

If I close my eyes
I could be anywhere.

Before now, even before the natives
none of this was here.

And before that
it was just space.

Da Emma, Montreal

I

We have trouble finding the restaurant
located in the former women's prison.

I wonder if I rob someone nearby if
they'll just take me there.

Addie reminds me it was a women's prison
and that we'd probably have to eat in different facilities.

I consult the map.

II

We receive a lesson in pasta
from a man who says he *knows* pasta.

He has studied it in every city.
So I wonder why he is a waiter

and then remember Paris where
the guidebook said, it is a proud profession.

He says fresh pasta can never be seved al dente.
We are believers and order the fettucini.

III

That's a *red sauce*
I want to tell you
about the dish
at the next table

which seems like
a mundane statement
which is why I've italicized
the words *red* and *sauce*

to emphasize the impressive
authenticity of the sauce.
Imagine if I'd said this
out loud.

Now that's a red sauce.
Do you get me?

IV

The agony endured here.
The regret and glimpses

of freedom from the tiny windows
where we eat pasta with mushrooms.

The Response Here to San Francisco's *Left Heart*

appears on a mug
in a tourist shop reading
I lost my ass in Montreal.

Writing On the Phone

People think I'm being one of *those people*
always on their phones texting and whatnot.
I wish there was a good way to communicate to them
I'm just being an artist in the twenty-first century.

Thoughts at Canadian Midnight

It has been a day.
If you could measure success

by the aches in your feet
then today has won.

A phone call has come saying that
Afrowipes have been invented.

There is a beer on the corner but
none in my stomach.

Coffee is the same here.
Unlike in other places where

it is different. I smell like
a person I would not want to

sit next to. Go ahead.
Smell me.

In too few hours
a van will take me away.

Free Transportation

You can borrow a bicycle anywhere in Montreal. Unlike in Los Angeles where someone else's bike does not belong to you.

Go Tell Aunt Rhody

Go tell Aunt Rhody the old gray goose is dead.
What if we treated humans the same way?

Go tell Aunt Rhody Uncle Henry is dead.
We'll cook him up for supper.

We'll cook him up for supper.
Foot in mouth.

Foot in mouth.
It's a cookbook.

It's a cookbook.
Soylent green is people.

Foot in mouth.
Go tell Aunt Rhody

Uncle Henry's foot
is in my mouth.

Underground City

You can be underground for
weeks in Montreal, never without food,
never without a place to shop
never coming up for outside air.

Unlike in Los Angeles where the
underground is occupied by roots
and failed basements.
Where if the palm trees don't

see you outside they
will miss you. They
will call your mother.

Quotes For the Back of a Future Book

Rick Lupert has done it again.
What he's done we don't know.
But surely something has been done.

Read this book or die trying.

Aww fuck it.

Old
Québec City

A Good Start

Because of a mistake
having to do with paperwork
we get to take the front row seats
formerly occupied by the
Filipino French ladies.
We wish them well as
our three hour window to
Quebec City widens like
an opening eye.

On the Way to Québec City

I

We stop for coffee in the middle of the province
That is we stop and I decide it is for coffee.

A French vanilla from a machine,
Gas Station Coffee Addie calls it.

I pay with a twenty and the girl
wonders if I have anything smaller.

I do not.
Another transgression of America.

II

As best as I can interpret the symbols
on the Canadian road sign, at the next
highway exit you can get gas, food, a
Christmas tree and a pack of American
Boy Scouts. I'd pull over but I already
have coffee and no knots to tie.

III

Haiku

Our driver's name is
Raymond Bernard but, of course,
we can call him Ray

My Longest French Conversation Yet

until we got to the part about whether
the iced tea can come unsweetened

when the waitress gave up and
switched to English.

It is like seeing how long you can
hold your breath before it all goes to hell.

Not a remarkable victory.
But a record none the less.

Not Prêt-à-Porter

I am wearing
socks with sandals.
I have become one of
those people who
should be judged
for doing such things.

Rain Kind of Kills
Old Québec City for Us

Everyone I know has left their umbrella
in the hotel so it's awning to awning
avoiding puddles as we can except for
the time my sandle-in-socked foot
goes right into one puddle, which I
don't notice as much as Addie's gasp
as she watches it happen.

I'll always have the memory of all
the surrounding oxygen going into
my wife, launching the era of
the slightly wet foot.

In Canada, if you are sick, they will heal you

unlike in America where you will be fined if you do not have health insurance.

Restaurant Madrid on Autoroute Jean-Lesage Between Québec City and Montreal

The place is surrounded by dinosaurs
Not real ones I think, for various reasons.
Unless they are standing very still.
I wouldn't want to stand like that
in the rain.

Juxtapose

The old and the new.
Two mohawked boys feign a jig
on the cobblestones of old Québec.
The old and the new.

Montreal
trois

Universality

On Rue St. Denis
where they make their own beer
on the premises

across the street
a venue called *Atmosphere*
No-one inside

A couple at the next table
move to a table farther away
leaving a mustard bottle

on their table
I pick up the bottle
Offer it to them

They laugh in French
A bottle of mustard
works in any language

The Live Spectacle

On Rue St. Denis
a tribe of thirty
white and black people

That is white shirts
and black pants
each with a flashlight

walk in unison
Synchronized flashlight pointing
All of them crouch

Of course we follow
They reverse direction
More crouch, a shout

Follow to building
Unison dancers on four balconies
The people shout *Juliette*

She bends
Lights pointed at her
The complete circus

Context

Addie recites the characteristic
of each beer in the beer sampler.
Of course I didn't realize this is what
she was doing when she started with
the word *hop*.

In the Dark

She remembers the
bathroom light switch
is on the outside
of the bathroom.

I do not.

It is a daily occurrence.
The door swings shut
and I, on the other side,
in need of rescue.

Different Tracks

Addie says the words "sleeping baby"
to which I reply "clumping bamboo".
We all have our priorities.

The Japanese Tea Ceremony

There are 100 rules to the ceremony
Each written as a poem

Typically the sound of drums and
air conditioning are not involved

So much is passed
during the silence

The guest is the most important
Still she will bow to apologize

for being served first
The utensils and bowls

are turned before use
They all have a face

The guest announces she
is drinking the tea

It is done with
three and a half sips

and an audible *slurp*
to finish

This is the sound
of respect

There is a hierarchy of guests
Though all humans are the same inside

Outside roles are left
outside

Everything is purified
Excuse me for going

before you

At Chez L'Épicier, Montreal

No reservation so seats at the bar
Watermelon cocktail makes it okay

Cabbage scented butter
A soup shot-glass for *amuse boucher*

Remind me to find out what
amuse boucher means

Cold cucumber soup
Red truffle oil croutons

The bar tender practices
golf swings between pours

A study in asparagus
Including goat cheese based

asparagus souffle
Cold and hot mix

Plates and spoons
Longer than they need be

House-made
kir

Canadian apple cider with
Canadian maple syrup

Chocolate club sandwich with
pineapple fries

House-made bread served
with cabbage scented butter

These are not the specials
This is every day

at chez
L'epicier

I want to ask our waiter
the bartender

If I die here
do I still have to pay

He wants me
to ask him

This is the détente
at dinner

A Difference

Electric hand dryers blow
faster and harder here
than anywhere in the world

Unexpected Meat

I tell Addie
Don't look to the right

which she immediately does
and sees the racks of lamb

Protruding bones
on the adjacent plates

Waiting for the Cirque to Start

Will anyone tall
sit in front of me?

Will the people behind me be upset
if I am propped up on my leg?

Couldn't they bring out just
one elephant?

The answer to all of these questions
is yes.

Except for the one
about the elephant.

During the Cirque

They do things with jump-ropes
that would have destroyed
your childhood

Farewell

The last poutine on our last night
in the same place as the first one on the first night.
I savor the gravy to remember its elements.
We will remember you Montreal with a
reenactment of your staple.

We will drive away tomorrow.
West to have every last moment in your province
before we cross the St. Lawrence into our homeland.
Due south to a rendez-vous in Syracuse where we
will regale them with tales of you, your Anglo-Franco
blend, your Inuit peace, your infectious excitement
at the strength and bravery if your Cirque performers.

You have your issues...the labor disputes that keep us
from the insects and the animals, your fifty-fifty desire
to emancipate yourself from the surrounding motherland.
But these are dwarfed by your people's genuine love for you.

You take care of everybody just the same. They've all got
an apple in their bowl and a Band-aid in the medicine cabinet.
You make sure of it. It's no wonder so many cross the river
and don't look back.

We will miss you Montreal, Québec, Canada.
We will not forget you. We will look for cheese curds
as soon as we get home.

départ du Canada

Leaving Canada

The water in Canada tastes good
unlike in Los Angeles where
there is no water to begin with.

Leaving Québec

We drive out of Québec into Ontario
The signs gradually change from just French
to English with French to just English.
It is sad because I like being in a place
where they speak French.

A sign up ahead reads *United States.*
It is sad.

A Sighting

I could swear I saw your forehead in a gas station
in Morrisburg, Ontario. It definitely had your shine.

You were wearing a more casual T-shirt than
I am accustomed to seeing cover your ink.

It occurred to me you are not as tall as your father.
Do you get that from your mother or did they have
you custom-made?

I wish you had told me part of your head
would be in Canada today. I would have
baked a cake.

In The Air Again

Flying over America
tired as the day I was born.
There are lights outside the plane.
Could be anywhere.

There is an hour until
we land on shaky ground.
It will be too dark to appreciate
a homecoming.

Too late to enjoy
the traffic-free ride home.
Probably traffic-free.
You never know in L.A.

The author, somewhere in Canada.

About The Author

Rick Lupert has been involved in the Los Angeles poetry community since 1990. He served for two years as a co-director of the Valley Contemporary Poets, a non-profit organization which produces readings and publications out of the San Fernando Valley. His poetry has appeared in numerous magazines and literary journals, including *The Los Angeles Times, Rattle, Chiron Review, Zuzu's Petals, Caffeine Magazine, Blue Satellite* and others. He edited *A Poet's Haggadah: Passover through the Eyes of Poets* anthology and is the author of twelve other books: *We Put Things In Our Mouths, Paris: It's The Cheese, I Am My Own Orange County, Mowing Fargo, I'm a Jew. Are You?, Feeding Holy Cats, Stolen Mummies, I'd Like to Bake Your Goods, A Man With No Teeth Serves Us Breakfast* (Ain't Got No Press), *Lizard King of the Laundromat, Brendan Constantine is My Kind of Town* (Inevitable Press) and *Up Liberty's Skirt* (Cassowary Press). He has hosted the long running Cobalt Café reading series in Canoga Park since 1994 and is regularly featured at venues throughout Southern California.

Rick created and maintains the Poetry Super Highway, a major internet resource for poets. (PoetrySuperHighway.com)

Currently Rick works as the music teacher and graphic and web designer for Temple Ahavat Shalom in Northridge, CA and for anyone who would like to help pay his mortgage.

Rick's Other Books

We Put Things In Our Mouths
Ain't Got No Press ~ January, 2010

A Man With No Teeth Serves Us Breakfast
Ain't Got No Press ~ May, 2007

I'd Like to Bake Your Goods
Ain't Got No Press ~ January, 2006

STOLEN MUMMIES
Ain't Got No Press ~ February, 2003

BRENDAN CONSTANTINE IS MY KIND OF TOWN
Inevitable Press ~ September, 2001

up liberty's skirt
Cassowary Press ~ March, 2001

FEEDING HOLY CATS
Cassowary Press ~ May, 2000

I'm a Jew, Are You?
Cassowary Press ~ May, 2000

MOWING FARGO
Sacred Beverage Press ~ December, 1998

Lizard King of the Laundromat
The Inevitable Press ~ February, 1998

I Am My Own Orange County
Ain't Got No Press ~ May, 1997

Paris: It's The Cheese
Ain't Got No Press ~ May, 1996

For more information:
http://PoetrySuperHighway.com/

www.ingramcontent.com/pod-product-compliance
Lightning Source LLC
Chambersburg PA
CBHW062005040426
42447CB00010B/1916